# INXS

## THE OFFICIAL INSIDE STORY OF A BAND ON THE ROAD

**St. Martin's Press**

# INXS

## THE OFFICIAL INSIDE STORY OF A BAND ON THE ROAD

INXS: The Official Inside Story of a Band on the Road.
Text copyright © 1992 Truism Pty Ltd. Yann Gamblin's photographs copyright © 1992 Truism Pty Ltd. Design copyright © 1992 Jonathan Goodman. All rights reserved. Printed in Hong Kong. No part of this book may be used or reproduced in any manner whatsoever without written permission except in the case of brief quotations embodied in critical articles or reviews. For information, address St. Martin's Press, 175 Fifth Avenue, New York, NY 10010.

Text by INXS with Ed St. John
All photographs by Yann Gamblin
except those at Wembley Stadium, July 13, 1991 by Andrew Southam and those on pages 25 (main picture), 27 (inset) and 71 (inset right) by Eugene Adebari.

This is a Jonathan Goodman book for Carlton Books Ltd

Designed by David Rowley, The Image,
10 Barley Mow Passage, Chiswick, London W4 4PH

Project Editor Carolyn Pyrah
Copy edited by Marilyn Inglis

Typeset by Pardoe Blacker Publishing, Lingfield, Surrey
Production Management in Hong Kong by
Mandarin Offset Ltd, Sixth Floor, 22A Westlands Road, Quarry Bay, Hong Kong
ISBN 0-312-08367-X

First edition: May 1992

10 9 8 7 6 5 4 3 2 1

*All veils and misty streets of blue*

*Almond looks that chill divine*

*Some silken movement*

*Goes on forever ...*

# foreword

*In a sense, we've spent most of our life on the road. Ugly long stretches of Australian two-lane highway, the band driving themselves in battered hire cars. . .thousands of miles of American freeways in buses with bunks and stereos and video screens. . .autobahns and* autostrada *and* autoroutes. *All the roads lead to a show, and that's all that really matters.*

*By the time we came to mount the* X-factor *tour in the second half of 1990, we figured we'd played something like 2,500 shows over the previous 14 years or so. Having taken touring to an extreme the last time around (the Kick tour consumed almost 18 months) we wanted to mount a more compact, efficient world tour. We were very proud of what we'd achieved with the X album, and we wanted desperately to get out and play it live, but we didn't want the shows to turn into a chore. We wanted this tour to be fun.*

*As you can see over the following pages, we succeeded. Thanks in part to a well-planned itinerary, and thanks also to a new, positive spirit within the band's ranks, we had the most enjoyable tour of our career. We played a few countries for the very first time — including Spain, Hungary, Norway, Sweden, Ireland and Mexico — and we also headlined before some of the biggest audiences we'd ever seen: 150,000 in Rio, 80,000 at Wembley Stadium, 90,000 in Cologne.*

*We completed the X tour in July 1991 feeling more unified and excited about the future than at any other time in our career. Almost as soon as we returned home to Australia we were back in the studio making album number eight — recording many of the songs that Andrew had written on the road. Suddenly, the idea of a holiday seemed ridiculous; we wanted to make some music together.*

*We'll have that album out in a couple of months — and then a whole new cycle begins. But in the meantime, we hope you enjoy this book. It documents a big and particularly enjoyable stretch of road.*

INXS

March 1992

**'Musically, I tend to be fairly adventurous. Michael and I**

# Tim Farriss

'Initially it was only Tim who believed we could go somewhere. He was always the car salesman, the one pushing us, getting us gigs and talking about us. We all just sat back and thought how good it was that we were living in a house together, playing gigs and getting free beer' (Garry Gary Beers).

'I think over the years my role has been a sort of team captain', says Tim Farriss of the contribution he makes to INXS. 'I basically put the band together in the first place, and very early on I was the manager as well with Kirk, dividing up the money after every gig.

'I've always been there for everyone, and even as we've matured and things have changed, that role has become an integral part of what we are.'

'Tim is like the ballast in the band', says the youngest of the brothers, Jon Farriss. 'He's the one who gives the band a bit of leadership, a sense of unity, and he'll usually project a very practical, logical view of everything. I think because he's the oldest Farriss brother, and he got married and had kids well before everyone else, he's a bit of a father figure for the band.'

Born in 1957, Tim's first experience of playing music was in a high school duo, then later in a band with Kirk Pengilly. This eventually led to the formation of the Farriss Brothers and INXS.

These days Tim Farriss doesn't manage INXS, but as the band's main guitarist he has played a vital part in the development of an original studio sound. Although he is rarely credited as a songwriter on INXS albums, he exerts an active influence on the band's musical identity.

'Tim personifies rock & roll', says Kirk Pengilly. He's the kind of guy who's capable of cracking a beer at 11 o'clock in the morning. On stage he's a real entertainer

in that archetypal rock guitar-player mould. We balance each other out really well.'

Tim's distinctively funky guitar riffs are a key part of INXS sound. On stage, they are transformed into lightning conductors as Farriss lights up the stage with electrifying bolts of performing energy. Totally absorbed in the power of the music, Tim Farriss live is a mesmerizing sight, forming with Kirk Pengilly a formidable frontline support team for Michael Hutchence.

'We assumed these natural positions on stage years ago', says Tim, 'with Michael in the middle and Kirk and I on either side. Kirk and I have been playing together for such a long time, and we've always had the attitude that whatever we did in music, it should entertain people.'

Tim Farriss and Kirk Pengilly form a perfect pair as the two frontline melody men in INXS, and they're firm friends offstage too. It's probably just as well, because they are often found handling the band's publicity chores.

'Yeah, I've done it reluctantly, let me assure you', says Tim. 'Kirk and I seem to get lumbered with it because Garry and Jon don't particularly enjoy interviews and Andrew doesn't have the time as he's always writing.

'I really hate it that I'm the responsible guy. I'd rather be the guy that nobody can get out of bed.'

But somehow, Tim Farriss' life has never left much time for sleeping in. Tim married his wife Buffy in 1981 – back in the days when INXS were paying their dues with a roster of virtually non-stop touring and recording. Tim and Buffy live in Sydney with their two sons, Jake (born in '87) and James (born in '82).

'When we first got married I was still on the dole. When we had our first child I was still only receiving the equivalent of the dole from being in the band. Plus we started to do really extensive international tours when my first kid was really young – and believe me, there was no money around then for me to take my family along.

'Now that I could afford to take the kids, James is firmly entrenched at school, he has his friends in Australia and his life is there. I can't just whip him out of there for my benefit, although we all went over and spent three months living in London for the first leg of the X tour. We had a nice house overlooking the Thames at Chelsea Harbour and if I was playing somewhere close like Paris, I'd fly back home for the night.

# are always the ones who want the records to be totally out there, you know. Like we want to go all the way, all the time. I think if we had our way we'd be a slightly more obnoxious, full-on kind of band.'

'It's funny because now we're a lot older and I hear the other guys saying that their wives are having children and they want some time off and it's like, "oh really? I feel like working".

'But seriously, I went through so much pain and anxiety through being away from my family for months on end that I couldn't possibly mind anyone else having whatever thay want when it comes to family.'

Tim Farriss is a straightforward and genial man who seems utterly unaffected by fame. Dedicated as he is to INXS and everything the band does, he's an essentially private person who avoids attention whenever possible.

'If I go out during the day I try very hard not to stand out', he says. 'I mean Michael, just by being Michael, tends to stand out – but I try to be incognito, you know. I'll wear a cap and sunglasses and try to look as inconspicuous as possible, and that works well. But if I take the cap off and let my hair fall out then I'm signing autographs within five minutes.

'I seem to have become a lot less sociable in the past couple of years. I used to like to go out and party after a gig but quite often now I feel amost. . .hemmed in by any sort of crowd. I've been the focus of all that attention for two hours and I feel as if I have just nothing left to give anyone.

'To be honest, my favourite thing to do after a gig is to go back to my hotel room and just hang out, maybe watch a bit of TV with one of the guys and order some room service.'

Tim is justifiably proud of the achievements of the band he formed in Sydney in 1977. To hear him speak of future projects – more albums, more tours – it's clear he believes the best years are still to come.

'I've reached a point – I think we all have – where we don't give a damn about what others say or do any more', says Tim. 'I just know about my life and what I have to do – and I want to get on with it.'

# Kirk Pengilly

'**K**irk can be really funny on stage sometimes. He'll do this move across the stage where you'd swear to God he's not looking. You realize that you'd better get the fuck out of the way because he'll just clean you up. He has this wild look in his eye. . .and at moments like that I wonder what planet he's on. It's like, "do I know this guy?" ' (Tim Farriss).

For Kirk Pengilly, the INXS experience began not in 1979, when the band finally agreed on a name and began working in earnest towards their first record deal, but eight years earlier. 1971 was the year Kirk and his best friend at school, Tim Farriss, formed their first band.

'The band was called Guiness', laughs Kirk, 'and we basically had it for most of our high school years and about two years after we left. It was a band that meant a lot to me because I wrote all the songs and I was the singer as well. We actually auditioned Jon as drummer at one point but he was only nine years old so we kicked him out.'

Guiness eventually split up – but within a few months Tim contacted Kirk with an interesting idea: amalgamate the talents of Tim and Kirk with the best elements of his younger brother Andrew's band – Michael Hutchence, Garry Gary Beers and Andrew himself. The only factor needed to complete the line-up was a drummer, and although Jon was still very young – 16 by then – he was more successful at his second audition. In March 1977 the six-piece band that would become INXS was born.

'I absolutely believe that you create your own reality', says Kirk, 'but when I look back on the way we came together it's just amazing. You know, Michael had been living in Hong Kong and LA for years and just happened to land in the same school class as Andrew. I'd moved from Melbourne, the Farriss brothers had moved from Perth. . .and we all just wound up in the same place like it was meant to happen.'

In the years since the formation of INXS, Kirk Pengilly has developed a unique position within the band. As saxophonist, guitarist and principal backing vocalist he contributes a large proportion of the band's distinctive melodic sound. Offstage, he also takes a keen interest in the band's publicity and PR, accepting responsibility for many of the interviews and hand-shaking chores that come with touring. He takes this position in the band very seriously – and tackles his work with exemplary enthusiasm: in the words of Jon Farriss, 'Kirk's a really nice, boy-next-door kind of guy.'

'I don't seem to get as exhausted by touring as some of the guys – so I don't have a problem with it. It can be a bit of a drag to do "meet-and-greet" sessions with record retailers and radio people before every gig. . .but they serve a very important purpose. I think if people

## 'I know it's probably a little

leave those things feeling good about the band because you bothered to talk to them then they're going to sell your records with a lot more enthusiasm. It's just good business practice, really.'

As even a cursory glance at the record books would show, INXS have achieved an incredible amount in their relatively brief history. Not only have they recorded seven albums and released a live LP, they have also given 2,500 live performances. Tackling the world from a country as remote as Australia has required an extraordinary commitment from all members of the band, and to hear Kirk Pengilly tell it, it's a commitment which only strengthens with time.

'I actually think we're more unified now than we've ever been', he enthuses. 'We took a year off after the *Kick* tour, and as a consequence it was quite stressful and challenging when we regrouped to make *X*. But we emerged from making that album, and from the *X* tour, feeling stronger and more unified than ever before.

'That year off was really important to our development, because it was literally the first time we'd had the time and space to get our lives together.' Kirk spent much of his extended vacation getting to know his daughter April, born in 1988. 'We hadn't previously had the opportunity to develop as individuals because we were always together and always working. It was like taking six lions who had been locked in a cage together for 12 years. . .and just letting them go.'

More frightening still, of course, was that the six lions were put back into the cage after a year of freedom when the time came to record the *X* album.

'There was a lot of tension when we first came back together. We'd all gone off and done other things so there was a period when we had to re-establish where we all sat with one another. And I guess you have those nagging questions like "Will it work? Will the magic still be there?"

'But those doubts were dispelled pretty quickly. *X* was a hard album to make, but by the time we'd finished we were all very proud of it. There are a lot of musical subtleties in it that weren't immediately noticeable which revealed themselves with time – and we felt we'd made progress.

'INXS keeps evolving and changing. Individual roles in the band shift around, members' input into different areas is always increasing or decreasing. It's very fluid, but it's also very volatile because we're six very creative people. And right at the moment we're all pulling in the same direction.'

**unfashionable to say this, but I have to confess that I really like touring – and I really love doing all the stuff that goes with being in the band. I like meeting people, I like the whole buzz of travelling and playing.'**

# Michael Hutchence

## 'I really don't consider myself to be any different from anyone else, and I don't expect to but I could have ended up in the audience just as easily.'

'I love being famous', says Michael Hutchence with typical candour. 'It's like a totally Freudian thing – it makes me feel wanted and loved and noticed. Anyone would want that, wouldn't they?'

There is no doubt about it – Michael Hutchence *is* famous. INXS's charismatic lead vocalist has entered a realm of international stardom that few singers or musicians ever achieve. He's become a genuine cultural icon.

But if Michael Hutchence enters the 90s a superstar, he's a fascinatingly low-key one. While acknowledging the pleasures of wealth and fame, he is also refreshingly down-to-earth in his day-to-day behaviour.

Says Jon Farriss, 'On stage Michael is expected to be absolutely incredible every night – like he's this super-human being who can whip huge crowds into a frenzy and hold 25,000 people in the palm of his hand. Off-stage he's expected to revert instantly to being totally normal. . .It's a very extreme situation he's in and I think he handles it in a very cool way.'

'It would be stupid of me to pretend that singing with INXS isn't exciting – because it is an unbelievable thing. It's so good, it's beyond words; it's ridiculous to even attempt to quantify it. But perhaps just to deal with it I find myself saying "it's no big deal, this is just what I do."

'I don't really believe I'm there, to be honest. I find it very, very weird that I'm on stage in front of thousands of people. On one level I'm completely involved with what's happening, but on another level I'm completely cut off from it, like I'm in a bubble.'

Observing Michael's lifestyle provides a revealing insight into his attitude to his work and life. When not on tour, he leads the life of an international nomad, visiting friends and living for short periods in places as diverse as Hong Kong, Los Angeles, London and France.

But he doesn't necessarily move with the international celebrity jetset – in fact that is a world he openly despises. Instead, Michael lives the life of a dedicated bachelor nightclubber – dancing, meeting people, staying out late. In a most unselfconscious way, the boy just wants to have fun.

'I'll very happily admit that I really enjoy going to clubs', says Michael with a grin. 'I mean, straight after the show at Wembley Stadium I headed out to a club. I do it most nights I'm on tour, so I guess I have a lot of stamina, although I find that if I overdo it, it is to the detriment of my health.

'But I don't go out as a "rock star", with an entourage of photographers and bodyguards and hangers-on. I go as myself, like I'm any other person going out, and I usually find that people respect that. I never do that thing Prince and Madonna do where they clear a private area of the club and have these huge guys standing guard. I just blend into the crowd.

'To me, clubbing is a way of staying in touch with what's really happening. I know it isn't always the most professional thing for me to do after a gig, but I personally can't bear the thought of being a professional. I mean, I think I deliver the goods when it comes to this band, but the thought that I'm doing this as a career really revolts me. I know that sounds perverse, but I'm a perverse person.'

Yet in between the travelling and the partying, Michael Hutchence has packed in more work during the life of the band (seven albums, two feature films and innumerable tours) than most people accomplish in a lifetime.

The *Kick* tour saw the birth of Michael Hutchence as a world-class live performer, but since the culmination of that tour in 1988, he has made equally impressive leaps in his abilities as a songwriter and singer. He credits the year-long break he took from INXS after the *Kick* tour and his involvement with the experimental dance band Max Q for this growth.

## be treated any differently. I've wound up singing on stage for a living,

'Prior to that, I don't think I'd really been my own person in a creative sense', he says. 'I'd never been able to pick and choose what I wanted to do or where I wanted to go, but in that 12-month period I took control of all that. I wrote and recorded an album with Max Q, and made a film as well. I found it incredibly liberating. The whole exercise gave me faith in myself as an artist, it gave me confidence that I was capable of doing something outside INXS.

'I had so much life and spirit in me after that year. I felt it was the best thing I'd ever done, not just for me but for INXS. I'd never really thought of myself as a musician before that. My contribution to INXS had been quite naive in a lot of ways, but through my other experiences I found I was capable of so much more. I came back feeling very refreshed and excited about where we could take INXS.'

The beginning of 1992 sees Michael Hutchence immersed in the recording of the eighth INXS studio album – and sounding more enthusiastic than at any other time in the band's career.

'We're making a harder, more extreme record this time around', says Michael with a slightly maniacal grin. 'X was maybe a little bit polite, like it was all woven together very smoothly. But this time we're taking each song as far as it'll go. We're not trying to follow anything up or pretend to be anything we're not. We're just following our instincts.'

'**A**ndrew would make a good psychological case study for somebody. He's a deep thinker, the old Andrew' (Tim Farriss).

Andrew Farriss is perhaps the most enigmatic element in INXS. For a start, he is the band's principal songwriter, creating – often with Michael Hutchence – some 70 per cent of the material and certainly every one of their biggest hits.

In the recording studio, Andrew plays many parts and approaches this meticulous, time-consuming work with a quiet, intense determination that sometimes sits at odds with the more buoyant, playful style of the rest of the band.

Andrew's affinity with the recording studio extends beyond the confines of INXS; for several years he has also played an active part in the career of Australian

# Andrew Farriss

singing star (and one-time INXS backing vocalist) Jenny Morris. Andrew has co-written songs on all three of Jenny's albums, and produced her second LP, *Shiver*.

But if Andrew Farriss is at home in the studio, he is notorious for showing far less enthusiasm for his touring commitments with INXS. 'My problem with it is that I don't like travelling to play', he explains. 'I love travelling for a holiday, and I love playing music if I'm able to go home every night – but I don't like combining the two. You never get to stay in one place long enough to get immersed in the culture.'

'Andrew is certainly the member of the band who least enjoys touring – but then again I think he probably exaggerates his feelings about that because I've often looked across at him on stage and he's having a fucking great time,' says Jon Farriss.

Kirk Pengilly comments, 'In a musical sense Andrew is very important on stage. He provides a lot of the ambience, the layers and the textures in the music. He's funny live, actually – of all of us he's the least inclined to stick to the format of a song. If he's a bit bored with a particular arrangement he'll just move outside the boundaries. He might have a really important keyboard line to play and instead he'll just pick up the harmonica and blow into that. It's like, "what the *hell* is he doing this time?" '

Yet watching INXS on stage, it's hard to believe that Andrew is possibly the key creative member of the band. Sitting at the back playing a combination of keyboards, guitar and harmonica – often looking as deliberately inconspicuous as possible – he is rarely the focus of attention. In many ways this suits him just fine.

'We have very clearly defined roles and positions on

'**Prior to the *Kick* tour I'd never written on the road – mainly because I didn't have time, I guess. But with *Kick* I started writing with a guitar, and I was**

stage', he says. 'I started off being put up the back because my keyboard rig was so big and heavy. There was no way it could be fitted down the front in your average Australian pub. I guess I used to sometimes wonder why it was that I wrote most of the band's music yet I sat up the back, but it's something that seems to work naturally and there's absolutely no argument about it these days.

'There was probably a time when we all used to get a little bit sensitive about the fact that Michael was always getting the attention while the rest of us were a bit anonymous. But over the past three years or so we've seen that fame go from being enviable to being something you wouldn't ever want, and to that extent I think I'm happy not to be the focus of people's attention. Nobody likes to feel left out and ignored. . .but nobody likes being under a microscope either.'

Radically different though they are, Andrew Farriss and Michael Hutchence have been firm friends since they first met at a Sydney high school in the early 70s. It was there that they formed their first band and began what has now become one of the most successful

## kind of proud that I'd taught myself to do that.'

songwriting partnerships in contemporary music.

'I can't say that it was really obvious in those days that Michael was going to be a star', recalls Andrew. 'He was simply this guy I'd met at school who was a friend, and as time has gone by I still think of him like that. Of course along the way he's become incredibly good at his art, but that hasn't changed the relationship.'

Andrew admits that in recent years it hasn't been as easy to maintain the partnership. Between the band's intense touring commitments and the fact that Michael now spends much of his time living outside Australia (Andrew lives in Sydney with his wife Shelley and their young daughter), it isn't always possible to get together.

'Let's face it, Michael is not the most reliable person in the world', says Andrew with a resigned laugh. 'I've had to learn to be a little philosophical about the whole songwriting thing these days – and I certainly refuse ·to chase Michael around to write songs. If he calls me up, fine. If I call him and he doesn't return my call, that's fine too. All I know is that it only works if we both want to do it – and if not, I can always write a song by myself.

'Michael and I never took our songwriting relationship that seriously. It was just something that happened and we took it in our stride. But very recently we've learnt to value it a bit more because we've seen some fantastic results from it over the years. I hope it's something we can hang onto.'

In the meantime, Andrew has discovered a new way to relieve the boredom of touring and maintain his songwriting output. He now takes a suitcase complete with keyboard, sequencer and tape recorder on tour, and can often be found in his hotel room writing songs.

'Originally, I think the idea was that if I wrote on the road it would stop me from going nuts – because I get very bored on tour. But I found it was also a really good way to make use of all that time that might otherwise be wasted. I wound up feeling more productive and less frustrated, and the best thing of all was that when I finally got off the road I didn't have to start writing for the new album because I'd already done it.

'The first song to be released from all the songs I wrote on the X tour was *Shining Star*, which I wrote in Berlin, then we recorded it in London the day after Wembley Stadium. Funnily enough, it's about touring.'

## 'My forté, and therefore my role in the band,

# Garry Gary Beers

**B**assplayer Garry Gary Beers is the oldest – and perhaps the quietest and most reclusive – of the six members of INXS. He rarely grants interviews, and takes a deliberately low profile both in videos and on stage. For Garry Gary Beers, there is only one important task – playing bass in one of today's hottest rhythm sections.

'I think it's great that one of the most memorable things about INXS sound is the rhythm', says Garry. 'Obviously you remember the singing and other things as well, but people are always mentioning our rhythm patterns, and particularly Jon's drumming, all the time.'

Garry Beers' own distinctively rhythmic basswork is a key element in the INXS sound – but he's not one to blow his own trumpet. On stage he appears deliberately to avoid the spotlight as he concentrates on his contribution to the often complex musical structures that underpin the band's music.

'When I go and see other bands play live, or see them on TV, I'm always amazed to see bassplayers wandering all over the stage paying no particular attention to what the drummer is doing', says Garry. 'When I'm on stage there's only one place to be, and that's right next to Jon's kit.'

'I love Garry because he's always been rock-solid. You always know exactly where he's at and you know that he won't fly off on some passing fad or interest. He's not the kind of guy who changes his mind about who he is. He's a bassplayer, you know. He loves it and he's very good at it' (Jon).

'I don't like going down to the front of the stage – partly because I'm a bit shy, but mainly because I believe my job is to play as tightly as I can – and try to have a

good time doing it. I really get off on my instrument.'

But according to Kirk Pengilly 'Garry is a real practical joker. On stage he's always doing things that the audience would never see – like flicking plectrums at the back of Tim's head. He provides a kind of on stage comic relief for the band.'

Success with INXS – and with his part-time 'holiday band' Absent Friends – has certainly brought its rewards for Garry Beers. For the past three years he has lived on a large farm 90 minutes' drive north of Sydney, sharing the property not only with the INXS concert stage (it lives in a spare shed when not in use) but with his wife Jodie who he married in early 1991, midway through the X tour.

Garry approaches his recording and touring work with an impressive dedication and professionalism – but he freely admits that the early days of INXS weren't quite so exemplary.

'We came from nothing, in many respects, and we've had to work incredibly hard for a very long time – and that's given us a particular attitude to life. I think we're all very realistic about who we are and what we represent. We don't get precious about things.'

Garry says that after all the years of virtually non-stop touring and recording with INXS, personal relations between the band members are still as strong as ever. It is this camaraderie, and the obvious musical compatibility of the six players, that keeps the band alive.

'When we're touring we still really enjoy each other's company – but we've also learnt to respect one another's privacy. I mean, I spent years sharing hotel rooms with Andrew. It was like being married to the guy because believe me, when you share a room with

**is my ability to lock into what Jon is doing. I think we have an almost psychic connection in that respect. I've learnt to take my lead from him rather than try to impose something on him.'**

someone you get to know everything about them. And we all know each other that well.

'We're quite capable of having arguments too', says Garry with a laugh. 'We've had some beauties, particularly after gigs, because we're passionate about what we do and can get very critical of ourselves. . .But generally our discussions are very constructive. We're united by a common goal – to be as good as possible.'

United by a common goal though they are, INXS is made up of six very different people, with widely varying musical tastes. Garry Beers is renowned within the band for his traditional musical leanings – functioning as a counterweight to the more contemporary impulses of other members.

'I think it's great that we all have different tastes in music', says Garry. 'Michael is into a lot of contemporary dance music and rap at the moment, whereas I really hate most of that stuff. I like a lot of older things that he

probably hates – but that's fine.

'With the new album that we're recording at the moment we're really excited with the music that's coming out. We're all producing it, which is something we'd never allowed ourselves to do together. I guess we never had the faith in ourselves. . .I think we're beginning a whole new chapter for INXS.

'We want to really immortalize ourselves over the next few years. I think we've reached the heights as a touring band, we've certainly hit a lot of peaks in terms of record sales in different places, and we're really proud of those achievements.

'But right at the moment we're not entirely convinced that we've made the best record we're capable of making. We want to be remembered for our music, not for our lifestyles or our partying or our relationships. We want to make some albums in the 90s that'll blow the tits off everyone.'

# Jon Farriss

**'Drumming is a very no-bullshit activity. It's not a flashy spotlit performance thing, it's just a real musician's job where you sit look or what you say, it comes down entirely to what you do.'**

**J**on Farriss – the youngest member of INXS born in 1961 – is not your average drummer. For a start, he defies the conventions by being both good-looking *and* articulate. He's also very musical; in recent years he has put considerable effort into developing his talents as a songwriter, with the result that the *X* album contained two of Jon's co-compositions (*Faith in Each Other* and *Disappear*). But ultimately the single factor that sets Jon Farriss apart from the pack is his remarkable talent. Combining a natural rhythmic flair with an advanced understanding of state-of-the-art drum technology, Farriss is indisputably one of the finest drummers in contemporary music today.

'Jon is a fantastic drummer, a total motherfucker. I don't think I'm being biased when I say that I believe he's the best drummer in the world', says Garry Gary Beers.

Kirk Pengilly acknowledges that Jon is the member of the band who provides a really solid basis for the music. 'I see him as being a little like Scotty on the Starship Enterprise, you know, holding the ship together, running the engine'.

Jon Farriss is very modest about his abilities – but he does admit that as a rhythmic backbone for INXS, he has landed himself a particularly high-pressure job.

'It can get pretty stressful when you're playing live', says Jon. 'A lot of the songs are very mentally and physically demanding for me to play, and I guess I can also become very conscious of the fact that there are tens of thousands of people out there in the audience who all have expectations of what we can deliver. I definitely feel that we owe them the best show we can possibly put on.

'The worst part for me is in the minutes just before we go on stage – particularly the last few seconds when I'm sitting there at my kit waiting to count the first song in. In a sense it's a bit of a relief once we actually start playing. It's like "now we can start having some fun".

'I might add that I really do love playing live, having the music blasting out at the volume that it is and just the whole atmosphere of all these people being excited and together. It's a very stimulating thing. Particularly when we're sounding good it's almost like a religious experience.'

Jon sees himself not as a star performer on his own, but as an integrated part of the INXS rhythm section that also includes Garry Gary Beers and Andrew Farriss.

'On stage, I see the three of us as being one half of the equation', he says. 'We're like a planet that Michael,

## behind the kit and play as well as you can. It doesn't matter how you

Tim and Kirk can orbit around – and of course each side needs the other to work. We're the base, and we're not really in a position to go anywhere either literally or metaphorically. We lay the basis for the other guys to decorate melodically.'

Jon sees his musical relationship with Garry Gary Beers as being particularly crucial to INXS trademark sound. 'We take what we do very seriously', he says. 'We often get together to work out new ways of doings stuff, just constantly trying to make our musical relationship more perfect.

'There's so much that we've developed over the years that's kind of extra-sensory, that's based on intuition. We can just look at each other on stage without even making an expression. . .and the next minute we're both doing some amazing little thing. It's the sort of thing that's probably too subtle for 95 per cent of the audience to even notice, but it's something we just privately get off on. Right after that we'll usually get the giggles because we can't believe this shit's going on.'

Jon Farriss began his life with INXS as the band's baby – at 16 he was still at high school when they started playing live together on a regular basis. He's also the youngest of the three Farriss brothers, but claims that fraternal relationships have very little bearing on the band's internal dynamics.

'Obviously the three of us do have a particular bond that only brothers can have', he says, 'but it isn't really relevant in the context of the band. If anything we're three very different people who are just as likely to disagree on things. Andrew and I have a very intense relationship. We're both very creative people and I think we both have trouble articulating things except through our music. So we're prone to clash verbally over certain things. . .and often it turns out that we're saying the same thing. In terms of musical direction we're actually rather similar.'

These days Jon Farriss – who only very recently married his American wife, Leslie, sees the entire membership of INXS as his brothers. And as with any family, he sees the band sticking together for a very long time to come.

'We've never once had a line-up change in this band – and I can't imagine that it would ever occur', says Jon. 'We're like a family now, and like any family I guess there have been times when you may wish that one person or another wasn't there. . .but you could never seriously consider life without them. I think this band would split up before we kicked anyone out. . .and we're not about to do that either.'

# THE  **X** TOUR

In October 1990, INXS embarked on a 10-month world tour in support of their seventh studio album, *X*. The *X* album and tour occurred at an important point in the history of the band. At the time of its release the album title was an enigma – did *X* stand for ecstacy, did *X* mean multiply or did *X* mark the spot? In retrospect, well after the release of the album and the completion of the tour, it is possible to understand that *X* symbolized a crossroads. ▶

18

But let's wind back for a moment to 1979, the year that an upstart Sydney pub band called the Farriss Brothers decided on a name change to INXS. In the same year the band acquired a manager, C. M. Murphy, and within 12 months had recorded their self-titled debut album.

Over the next four years INXS toured Australia relentlessly, playing six and sometimes seven nights a week. They also found time to record three more LPs – *Underneath The Colours*, *Shabooh Shoobah* and *The Swing* – which attracted an increasingly loyal home-territory following. *The Swing* entered the Australian charts at Number 1.

Thanks to some exploratory international touring, and the encouraging success of singles like *Original Sin* and *The One Thing*, INXS had also developed the beginnings of a strong market in the UK, Europe and the USA. By the end of the American leg of *The Swing* tour in 1984, INXS was able comfortably to sell out the Los Angeles Palladium.

With the release in 1985 of their fifth album, *Listen Like Thieves*, INXS had reached the top of the pile in Australia but was faced with conquering the rest of the world. So with the same combination of live performance prowess and extreme determination that had worked at home, the band took to the world's concert

**Below: taking a break with manager C. M. Murphy. Bottom: all dressed up and about to go on stage in Europe. Right: the first release of energy at the start of a show.**

stages. From August 1985 until the end of 1986, INXS toured virtually non-stop. The strategy worked, delivering the band their first US Top 10 hit (*What You Need*) and platinum sales in several countries throughout the world.

The beginning of 1987 saw INXS back in the studio recording for the second time with British producer Chris Thomas. Six months later the band emerged with *Kick*, the album that was to guarantee them success as an international supergroup. Thanks to singles like *Need You Tonight* (their first US Number 1), *Devil Inside* and *Never Tear Us Apart*, the album turned into a multi-platinum hit the world over, prompting an unprecedented 16 months of world touring. The *Kick* tour finally ground to a halt in the closing stages of 1988.

'By the end of that tour we were completely exhausted and burnt out', says Garry Gary Beers. 'I mean, we'd done *Listen Like Thieves*, toured on that for ages, recorded *Kick* straight away and then toured for 16 months. . .the *Kick* tour escalated as it went along. It started out fairly modestly and gradually just got bigger and bigger.'

'Towards the end of the *Kick* tour, I guess we started to feel a little bitter because we were tired and we'd had enough,' adds Kirk. 'We were probably stupid to feel that way, because the whole world was going nuts for the album, but we were just feeling the pressure.'

'I don't necessarily buy this "burnt out" business', cautions Andrew. 'I think we were tired, sure, and some of us, like Jon, were naturally physically fatigued. We'd been working for over two years straight so we needed, and

deserved, a good holiday. For me, more than anything else, there was a need to just wipe the blackboard clean. We had been working on the same music for so long and we just needed to empty our heads of that and

start again from scratch.'

Whatever the analysis, INXS clearly needed serious time out – so they took the first real holiday of their careers. For the best part of 1989, INXS simply ceased to be. As Kirk Pengilly puts it, 'For the first time since we'd left high school, we actually had the opportunity to function as individuals.'

Most band members took time during the break to engage in outside projects – Kirk Pengilly and Tim Farriss produced a young Sydney band, Crash Politics. Garry Gary Beers recorded and toured with a group of mates called Absent Friends. Jon Farriss wrote songs while Andrew produced and toured with singer Jenny Morris – and got married as well. Michael Hutchence formed and re-cored the one-off band, Max Q, and also took the opportunity to make his second feature film, *Frankenstein Unbound*.

'In a sense, INXS split up after the *Kick* tour', says Jon Farriss. 'We all sort of went "goodbye, I don't know when I'll see you again", and walked away from it. It was a wonderful break because it was the first taste any of us had ever had of real personal freedom.

'It was also the first time that any of us had felt in control of our own lives. Up until then we'd done things because we had to do them rather than because we chose to. So when we all got back together again it was a very conscious decision. We weren't fulfilling an

**Winter in London. Far left above: admiring a Harley Davidson. Above: Jon Farriss reflecting on the show in the washroom at Docklands Arena. Far left below: Kirk Pengilly and Tim Farriss in an impulsive moment in the Wembley Arena dressing room. Following pages: Kirk Pengilly at Wembley Stadium (page 24) and the band on stage in Europe (page 25).**

**INXS officially go on stage for the first time in nearly two years at the start of the *X* tour with a string of warm-up dates in Australia.**

obligation, we were doing it because we wanted to.'

'When you're constantly around one another – the way we'd been for 10 years, you really influence each other in so many ways', observes Michael Hutchence. 'On a long tour you can actually lose track of the differences between everyone and sort of merge into one person with the same tastes in music and clothes and everything.

'Of course when we all got back together again after a year it was like putting the band together from scratch. We came back as virtually new people, with new tastes, new interests and new friends.'

When the six individuals regrouped in late 1989 as INXS, it was immediately apparent that the band's internal dynamics had subtly changed. All six band members had used the break to spread their wings both personally and creatively, and several band members had taken the opportunity to write new songs. Kirk Pengilly remembers their first months back together as being somewhat tense and difficult.

'There was a lot of pressure on the band to deliver something as successful as *Kick*', says Kirk, 'and also an internal pressure as to whether the band would still work – so we went through a period of trying to re-establish where we sat with each other.

'It was quite a difficult album for us to make, although I think some of that might have been because we weren't getting on as well with Chris Thomas. But ultimately we were very proud of the album we made.'

With *X* complete, it was time to consider touring again and although the band was committed to the idea of playing live once again, there were fears amongst some members. Would they be able to recapture the joy of playing live again? After all those years on the road, could it still be fun?

'We were never in any doubt that we'd be able to cut it live again', says Garry Gary Beers, 'but I think we lost sight of why we were doing it towards the end of

the *Kick* tour. We needed an injection of new music to make us feel fresh again and sure enough, once we'd finished the album, we started to get excited again.'

'I think we were all a little scared that when we finally got back to playing after all this time off, we might find ourselves hating it after a week or two', adds Jon. 'But that never happened.'

There should have been no serious doubt that INXS would function again as a brilliant live band. But in an era of super high-tech stadium rock tours, the band realized that they would have to present their music at the highest production levels.

'When we all sat down to discuss the tour, we all agreed that we'd reached a level where we simply had to put on a great show', says Kirk. 'We realized that we were literally competing with Prince and the Stones and whoever else may be out there for bums on seats.'

After an initial rehearsal period, the *X* tour kicked off with a string of October warm-up dates in Queensland, Australia's tropical northern territory. Although these small-scale shows weren't nationally advertised, the fans flooded in from all over Australia to witness the first INXS shows in almost two years.

'Those warm-up dates were an interesting time', says

Andrew. 'They were just little clubs we were playing, with a very cut-down production, but that made me realize how far we'd come, how big we'd become. Finding ourselves on a small stage again was quite confronting, in a sense.'

### The X Tour in Europe
The first leg of the international tour began in Rotterdam, Holland on November 1, 1990 and continued through Belgium, Scandinavia, Germany, France, Italy and Britain (including four-night runs at Wembley Arena and Birmingham NEC) over a seven-week period. It concluded in Ireland on December 18, leaving the band just enough time to return home for Christmas.

'Europe is a very tiring place to play', explains Garry Gary Beers. 'Every day you're not just in a different city, you're in a different country with a different language, different currency, different record company people to meet. The first early tours through Europe were very exciting because it's a great place and you can have a lot of fun, but by the *Kick* tour it was kind of exhausting us. We just retreated into our little bubble and virtually ignored where we were.

The *X* tour begins with the band committed to making a big impact.
Far left and below: Michael Hutchence and Tim Farriss in Europe. Left: 'Starship Jon' at Wembley Arena, London.

'But when we went back to Europe with the *X* tour, we didn't have the same problems. We'd had time to recuperate, plus I think we were just in a better frame of mind. We were also a lot more selective about the gigs we were playing and it was basically an interesting time to be there. The Gulf War was just starting, there were borders crumbling in Eastern Europe. . .so there was

more to be conscious of, more to think about.'

Kirk Pengilly agrees. 'It was an exciting part of the tour because we hadn't played Europe for quite a long time. . .a lot of things had happened since we'd been there. *Need You Tonight* had been a huge hit in England, for example. We'd won awards there but we hadn't been back to soak all that up.'

Because of Tim Farriss' fear of flying, the band travelled between a number of the European venues by train. It was a welcome break from the daily round of airport lounges and pressurized cabins. Travelling by train in France presented its own difficulties, however. In unfamiliar territory the INXS entourage had considerable trouble finding the appropriate platform – and in Montpellier they all wound up walking over three sets of tracks to find it!

'Travelling by train was kind of romantic in a way', recalls Tim. 'Pulling up at a French provincial railway

**INXS playing to an ecstatic crowd in western Europe at the start of the Gulf War.
Far left: Andrew Farriss, rarely seen up front, holding the centre stage with Michael Hutchence.
Above: the band's three frontliners enjoying their rapport with the fans.**

station in a fleet of limos was different and fun — and the best thing about trains is that the six of us can sit in a compartment and *talk* to each other. Having six-way conversations in a plane is impossible.'

By the time the band hit the UK, the harsh winter of 1990-91 was really setting in. As INXS played their final show at Birmingham's NEC, the north of England was being hit by severe snowstorms. Two of the band's trucks were subsequently snowed in, so the first of two Glasgow shows had to be cancelled. The year — and this initial European leg — ended with concerts in Manchester, Paris and Ireland. In Dublin, Australian producer Mark Opitz recorded one of the shows at the

Point Theatre — a show eventually included in the *Live Baby Live* album project.

The six members of INXS flew home to their families, taking a welcome two-week Christmas break in the midst of a contrastingly hot Australian summer. For Garry Gary Beers, the January break was a perfect time to slot in a wedding. His fiancée Jodie had accompanied the band throughout the first European leg of the tour, but after January it was his wife who came along for the ride.

## INXS Takes X to the Americas

By January 11 it was time to embark on the American leg of the tour, a three-month expedition covering some 45 shows. The first port of call was Mexico City, where the band played three dates at the Palacio de los Deportes to 60,000 people, prior to appearances at the Rock in Rio in Rio de Janeiro, Brazil, and in Buenos Aires, Argentina. For the last of three incredibly successful Mexico City shows, the band donned sombrero hats during *Never Tear Us Apart*.

The band at Rock in Rio, Brazil. Left: Michael Hutchence and Jon Farriss while setting up for an audience of more than 150,000. Below: greeting the audience – 'Hello Rio'. Far left above: Kirk Pengilly and Andrew Farriss. Far left below: the band's reception in Rio doubles the expectations of Tim Farriss.

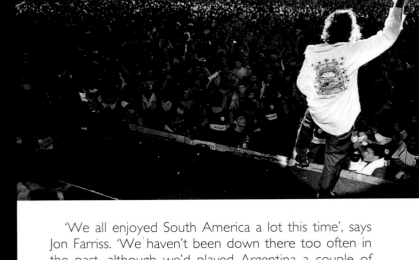

'We all enjoyed South America a lot this time', says Jon Farriss. 'We haven't been down there too often in the past, although we'd played Argentina a couple of times and that went really well again this time. Mexico City was great because we were the first international rock band to play in the city for something like 20 years. We were told the last band to play there was the Doors.'

Tim Farriss agrees. 'I think the South American shows were just wild. I particularly like Buenos Aires because it's just the most amazing, happening city and we all love it there. It's not a great place to be a vegetarian but we had a ball.'

Tim adds that the band took the opportunity to play a practical joke during the South American leg. 'We always have a lot of fun between ourselves on stage that nobody in the audience usually ever sees. On birthdays we like to play some kind of joke on the birthday boy – and in Buenos Aires it was Michael's birthday. We had a girl bring a birthday cake onto the stage in the middle of the set. . .and she was completely naked!'

But the undisputed highlight of the tour was the band's appearance at Rock in Rio before an audience estimated to be in excess of 150,000. 'It was an incredible event', says Jon. 'There were just so many amazing acts appearing there over seven or ten days that it was even exciting for the bands. We had Prince at the side of the stage for our set.

'The only problem I have with those things is that the audience has to sit through hours and hours of great music, so they tend to get a little jaded by it all. Like the night we headlined, we didn't come on stage until 2 a.m., so everyone in the audience was pretty drunk and exhausted. And let's face it, it wasn't easy for us to get to 2 a.m. completely straight either.'

From South America the band dropped into Los Angeles for several days, appearing at the American Music Awards and on the Arsenio Hall Show and slotting in a photo session with Herb Ritts. The very same day, INXS learnt that they had just won a BPI award (the UK music industry's most distinguished prize) as Best International Rock Group. Michael Hutchence was voted Most Popular Male Singer. On February 1 INXS

played for a secret club show at the famed Whiskey Au Go Go club (recorded live on radio) before jetting back east to Florida for a slow northward crawl through Georgia, Ohio and Philadelphia.

'We'd said for ages that we wanted to slot a few more club gigs into the schedule because they're kind of different and fun', says Michael. 'The Whiskey Au Go Go show was weird. We all kept looking at each other and

Far left above: Copacabana Beach, with Polygram flying the Welcome to Rio flag for INXS. Above: starting the day with champagne in Buenos Aires. Far left below: Tim Farriss, Michael Hutchence and Niki Turner, *X* tour publicist. Left: Jon Farriss backstage in Mexico wearing a sombrero for the final show at Palacio de los Deportes. Following pages: on and backstage at Rock in Rio.

laughing because here we were a few days after playing to 150,000 at Rock in Rio. . .and we were all crammed onto this tiny stage playing to a small room full of music industry people.'

At LA the band had picked up a twin-propellored Gulfstream jet for the American tour with British band the Soup Dragons (the support act). They immediately headed to Florida for the first official shows in Daytona, Miami and Tampa, then travelled to New York, setting up base at the Plaza Hotel from where they commuted to shows in Georgia and Philadelphia.

By mid-February, with war raging in the Persian Gulf, INXS descended on Madison Square Garden. 'That place is always a blast', says Garry Gary Beers. 'We sold it out, had a great show, and then you walk backstage and there's Keith Richards telling you he had a great time. It's the kind of stuff that could only happen in New York.'

Jon Farriss agrees, but says New York can be a hard city to play. 'It's a place that every band plays eventually, so the New York audience sees an incredible array of bands coming through. So they're maybe harder to please – and the other problem is that it's what we call a profile gig with lots of VIPs in the audience and critics going "c'mon, impress me". In those circumstances you can find that you try too hard.'

As it happened, the Madison Square Garden show was something of a disaster. Half the band's PA failed to

Above (main picture and inset): in LA to begin the North American tour. Top: Andrew Farriss enjoying a solitary beer while (centre) Shelley is with Garry Gary Beers and Jodie (also right) at Nassau Coliseum, New York.

**INXS continue the North American leg of the tour. These pages: Michael Hutchence holds the attention of tens of thousands of people. Following pages: (inset pictures) Michael Hutchence and Tim Farriss doing some poses in front of a fired-up crowd. (Main picture) offstage with Jon Farriss after a hard night's work.**

function properly, and the lighting system short-circuited, leaving two enormous smoke machines billowing clouds of smoke onto the stage for most of the set. 'It was totally ridiculous,' recalls Tim with a wry laugh. 'We could barely see each other.

'I have to confess that I don't really enjoy the profile gigs so much. In many ways I prefer it when we're playing a smaller town in the Midwest or something – and OK, there's nobody famous there but there are 15,000 really excited, honoured people who really appreciate the fact that you're there. They're not blasé or jaded. These are the gigs where you can really have a good time.'

If the Midwest was what Jon Farriss was after, he got what he wanted, and more, after New York. The tour proceeded on to Kentucky before heading north again through Michigan, Ohio and Indianapolis. The band commuted by jet to shows in New Jersey, Philadelphia,

Massachusetts and Connecticut. The shows – some of them recorded by Mark Opitz for *Live Baby Live* – went well, with the undisputed highlight being a show in Hartford. A Hartford radio station had run a competition asking listeners to submit an 'X-rated letter' detailing their ideal evening with INXS. One of the winners, an outwardly shy and retiring girl, attended the pre-concert drinks and chatted politely to the band. Once INXS took to the stage, however, the girl become possessed – ripping off her bra and dancing topless in the front row! As Kirk Pengilly diplomatically comments, 'It was a very funny and entertaining evening.'

This leg of the tour also saw several members of INXS taking up a new backstage pastime – rollerblading (similar to rollerskating). In New York, Kirk, Garry and Jon had all bought blades and pads – and pretty soon most of the band was engaging in this demanding activity between soundchecks and shows.

The band arrive in Australia and play to an exuberant home crowd, selling out the Sydney Entertainment Centre six times over. Right: Andrew Farriss. Below and far right above: Michael Hutchence. Centre: Kirk Pengilly. Far right below: Jon Farriss.

Following pages:
**Michael Hutchence
and Tim Farriss
(above) and
Andrew Farriss
(below) adlibbing
during an
Australian show.
Garry Gary Beers
(main picture)
making up for
Michael's loss of
voice at Memorial
Drive, Adelaide.**

Then an extensive tour through Canada saw the band bouncing back across the border into Chicago, Cleveland and Milwaukee en route.

'Canada is a very special place for us', reflects Tim Farriss, 'because they've always been really big supporters of Australian music and they've been terrific to us. *Kick* is one of the biggest-selling albums they've ever had – in fact it's a diamond album there. I believe a diamond album is ten times platinum, which is fantastic. To be honest, we didn't know there was such a thing.'

The American leg finished with a run down the West Coast, starting in Vancouver, going through Seattle and Portland, a detour to Utah, then on to California. Along the way most members of the band took advantage of excellent winter snow coverage to do some intensive skiing. As Tim puts it, 'We all got the skiing bug at the same time. Every available minute we had we were out on the slopes somewhere.'

The band completed the American tour with a handful of dates in California (Oakland, Sacramento, San Diego) as well as concerts in Phoenix and Las Vegas. In Las Vegas, Michael Hutchence organized six showgirls to dance behind the drum during the riser for *What You Need* – but forgot to tell the rest of the band. 'We all got such a shock,' recalls Tim Farriss. 'We turned around and there they all were, kicking their legs in the air. It was hilarious.'

But for Jon Farriss, San Diego – the last stop on the American tour – is the show that really sticks out in his mind. It was there that he had his first date with the girl he was to marry in 1992.

'I think I'll personally remember San Diego as the best

date of the tour', laughs Jon. 'I met Leslie the night before at a party and then I talked her into coming to San Diego for the gig. For some reason our audience was totally wild and crazy, so it was just a great gig.'

## X in Australia

Barely pausing for breath, INXS winged home in April 1991 to warm up to their first national Australian tour since the *Kick* juggernaut ground to a halt in late 1989. Spread out over three weeks, the tour took in Australia's five major capital cities, Perth, Adelaide, Melbourne, Brisbane and finally Sydney, where the band sold out the 12,000 capacity Entertainment Centre six times over.

'In many ways Australia is where we're at our most nervous', observes Kirk. 'I think it may be because Australia is where most of our friends still are, and we get a little selfconscious about that. You're up in front of people who've watched you grow up.'

Unfortunately, the Australian leg was not the highlight of the X tour. A matter of days before the band's first Perth show, Michael Hutchence began losing his voice. 'He was singing so brilliantly on the European and American legs of the tour', recalls Garry, 'but by the time we got to Australia he could barely talk. I think he

**Above: Michael
Hutchence giving
the fans his best
shot at Perth
Entertainment
Centre, April 1991.**

was really upset about it because he'd been really looking forward to showing everyone how well he was
singing. I don't think any of us had ever seen Michael so
excited about returning to Australia.

'I certainly wouldn't say the Australian shows were
bad. I don't even know if the audiences realized the
problem Michael was having, because we've learnt to
cover for each other so well in this band. But it frustrated us because we felt it could have been better.'

'I really shouldn't have done the Australian tour at all',
says Michael. 'My voice was in such bad shape that they
had to give me cortisone just to allow me to sing. But
that's pretty scary because it suppresses your immune
system, so you never really know how much damage
you're doing to your voice. Looking back on it, I think I
did do quite a bit of damage on that tour, and a year
later it's only just recovering.'

## The Last Leg

INXS remained in Australia for six weeks' recuperation,
during which time Michael's voice recovered its full
strength. At the end of the rest, the band headed back
to Europe and the UK to undertake a three-week tour
headlining summer festivals. One of the most enjoyable
legs of any tour, it concluded with a show at Wembley
Stadium, regarded by some members of the band as
their greatest show ever.

'We loved that leg of the tour so much – partly I
think because it was really short', recalls Tim Farriss.
'Three weeks is about the shortest international tour
we've done in something like six years. The result was
that everyone stopped worrying about the grind of
being on the road and just had some fun. We cut a few
old songs from the set which we'd been playing forever
and changed the song order completely on its head.

**Tim Farriss with
Niki Turner,
publicist,
sightseeing on the
River Thames in
London.**

Personally, I think it was the best tour I've ever had.

'The first gig was a warm-up show at a club in Ghent, Belgium. Initially the idea was that we would rehearse all afternoon, because we hadn't actually played together for six weeks. But we never got around to it because a couple of the guys were having problems with their gear. So we were all sitting around backstage saying, "What key is that in?"

'Then we got up and played this fantastic little gig. I remember Michael saying on stage that the audience was so close he could smell them, which was a line that got into all the newspapers the next day. But it was great, you know. The next gig was in front of 50,000 people.'

At the Rock Am Ring Festival in Nuremburg, Germany, INXS were joined by David A. Stewart for a rollicking rendition of *Suicide Blonde*.

'I love having other people play with us', enthuses Jon Farriss. 'It doesn't happen nearly often enough for my liking. We'd met Dave through Chris Thomas. He'd dropped into the studio in Sydney to say hi and I think Michael had met up with him in France on a couple of occasions. When he popped into our show in Germany, it was like "c'mon Dave, strap on that guitar."

'The audience didn't notice who it was for a minute until the guys on the cameras focused in on him and he was projected up onto the screens. He brought a great sense of camaraderie to the stage and he played this amazing acoustic guitar riff over the song which sounded fantastic.'

'Just before we went on', chimes in Tim Farriss, 'Dave told me he didn't care whether his guitar was turned on – he just wanted to get out there and do some great poses. He did, too. He's good to have around.'

More shows followed in Hungary, Austria, Switzerland, Holland and France – with the band celebrating Kirk Pengilly's birthday at a concert in Maastricht and then again on a bus trip to Amsterdam. The tour reached the UK and made its way north, first to Wembley Stadium and finally to Glasgow. 'I like stadium gigs', offers Tim Farriss. 'I guess there's a danger that it could turn you into this larger-than-life parody of yourself, but that isn't the effect it has on us. When gigs get that immense we actually get looser. We just think "fuck it, let's go for it".'

Well before the tour reached the UK, the band members realized that they were really enjoying being on the road together. 'With the *Kick* tour, I think we moved through life in a sort of blur', says Andrew. 'There was all this stuff happening to us but we really couldn't take it in and it wasn't until the tour finished that we were able to sit back and look at what we'd achieved. But with the *X* shows we were somehow able to take things in as we went along. It actually made the touring far more enjoyable and far less stressful.'

If the final European leg was generally enjoyable for INXS, the tension around the Wembley concert was intense. Not only were they headlining the biggest European concert of their career before an estimated 80,000 people, the concert was also being radio broadcast to a further three million people. On top of that a mobile van was recording the show for the *Live Baby Live* album project, and the entire event was also being filmed by 15 35 mm cameras for what was to be a concert film of the same name.

'Wembley was a very significant show for us', says

**Above and right: INXS play the biggest European concert of their career before an expectant crowd at Wembley Stadium, London.**

Garry Gary Beers, 'because we'd had to fight really hard to be accepted in England. We'd had to tour there year after year, slowly building up a live following, and the chart success has always been a bit elusive. I mean, *Kick* was in the UK charts for almost a year but it never reached Number 1. So to finally reach a point where we could sell out Wembley was just fantastic.'

'Just before the Wembley show, manager C. M. Murphy came up to Michael and me and told us he had this great surprise for us', recalls Tim. 'The surprise turned out to be a helicopter ride to the gig, if we did some interview he wanted us to do. And we were like "great surprise – no thanks" because we were so freaked out about the gig. There's no way I could have handled a chopper flight.'

A viewing of *Live Baby Live* concert footage shot at Wembley confirms beyond any doubt that the show was a resounding, triumphant success. It proved that INXS had lost none of their power as a live band; indeed they had elevated themselves to a new standard of excellence and musical inspiration. As if to underline their new commitment to their music, the band even managed to stagger to London's Metropolis studios the very next day to record *Shining Star*, which Andrew Farriss had written on the road in Germany.

'None of us could believe that we actually did that', laughs Tim Farriss. 'It was such a perverse thing to do the day after one of the most important shows of our career, but we were all just feeling right into the music again. We were all pretty wasted and out there, let me tell you, but the session worked.'

Instead of dissipating the band's energy, the X tour

**Wembley Stadium. Right: Garry Gary Beers backstage before the big night. Far right: (inset) Jon Farriss's fingers are protected with sticking plaster before the gig. (Main picture) Michael Hutchence singing late into the night as the crowd demands an encore.**

served to reunite INXS, kickstarting a new creative drive that will see the band recording great music well into the 90s. When the band returned to Australia there was no longer any talk of extended holidays. With producer Mark Opitz, the band immediately set about selecting and mixing tracks for the live album, then dived headlong into sessions for a new studio album.

'We faced a lot of challenges with *X*', says Kirk. 'It was a very stressful time, but we emerged from the making of the record and from the tour that followed feeling stronger and more unified than we'd ever been.

'The new album we're working on now shows how far we've come musically because it's more diverse in mood and feeling than anything else we've done – yet at the same time it's more unified.'

'We've been through some difficult times', agrees Tim Farriss. 'And right now there's real enthusiasm back in this band.'

Michael Hutchence
and Jon Farriss on a
riverboat trip down
the River Thames,
London, during the
second European
leg of the *X* tour.

# THE TOURING LIFE

'The thing about touring', says Jon Farriss, 'is that you're only on stage for two hours out of every twenty-four. So you spend the rest of the time getting there, preparing and waiting. But somehow I find that those two hours on stage make up for the other twenty-two hours of weirdness and boredom.'

Touring – that disorientating, arduous activity involving constant travel and literally hundreds of different hotels and ▶

backstage areas – is something INXS know about all too well. Touring has been a key factor in the international success of INXS – and one that for much of the band's career has been anything but glamorous.

'I suppose people imagine that INXS only ever travel around in limos staying at the best hotels and playing the biggest arenas', suggests Andrew Farriss. 'It makes me really angry when I hear that because even now, when I look back on the years of touring, the vast majority of those years weren't spent that way at all. They were in fact conducted in very threatening, depressing, confronting and emotionally draining situations where we were playing literally seven nights a week.

'We used to spend most of our early years in Australia driving from town to town; and the early days in America were just as bad, getting around in a clapped-out and overcrowded coach. One night our coach actually ran off the road because our driver fell asleep, so after that, for the next six tours or something, I used to stay up all night and sit beside the driver to make sure he stayed awake himself.'

'A lot of people assume touring is hugely profitable, but particularly when you're based in Australia, the cost of shipping people and stage gear all over the world really eats into your earnings', explains Kirk Pengilly. 'We were either running backwards or just breaking even right up until the second half of the *Kick* tour.

'Because of that we've tended to be pretty conservative in terms of our mode of transport and standard of

Far left above: Jon Farriss, Garry Gary Beers and Michael Hutchence arriving at a gig. Far left below: eating in some snatched hours, in Birmingham. Left: life's not always tough on the road – Jon Farriss with Leslie at Sydney Entertainment Centre. Above: there are occasional opportunities for sightseeing. Following pages: Judit Heidenreich (wardrobe) in Rio, sewing Michael's shirt (worn at Wembley Stadium).

**Below and left above: Michael Hutchence partying with best friend
Elle MacPherson (model) and Kylie Minogue. Left below: Karen
Hutchinson, Tim Farriss, Jon Farriss and David Le Bolt.
Following pages: Niki Turner with the band on the Thames.**

accommodation. We've slowly improved our comfort level every time we've done a tour, but we're still not really extravagant.'

The members of INXS are acutely aware of the fact that for many ordinary people, the touring life doesn't sound all that bad. 'Look, in many ways we have a very fortunate life', agrees Andrew Farriss. 'We travel to lots of incredible places, we stay – these days at least – in luxurious hotels, we play before all these adoring fans and we take home a bit of money. I'm sure a lot of people must wonder what the problem is.

'All I can really offer by way of explanation is that in order to have all those things we sacrifice a lot. For a start not just our personal privacy, but our entire private lives. For most people, their families and friends and homes are what their lives are all about. For us, touring all the time, our work becomes our life and that's obviously a huge compromise. We've been successful, but at a price; we've given a large part of ourselves away.'

'My problem with touring', says Michael Hutchence, 'is not the actual touring itself, but the fact that you can't do anything else. Eighteen months is a huge chunk out of your life, really, and you can get to the end of it and wonder what you've accomplished. But generally my attitude to touring is that I don't mind doing it if there's a genuine demand from people for us to play. I just hate going round and round in circles.'

As Jon Farriss says, touring is not just the excitement of standing on stage before 25,000 screaming fans. It's also all the other stuff that happens before and after.

'We never really get sick of playing, but there are so many hassles surrounding the show and that's what grinds you down. It can often be a relief to get on stage because it's the only time you can't be interrupted, where you're not obliged to meet anybody or do anything, except play.'

When INXS first started mounting tours of the USA and Europe in the mid-80s, the band invariably travelled by road, clocking up thousands of miles in buses of various shapes and sizes. These days they normally travel by aeroplane – usually a private jet. Yet for many members, the perceived glamour of private planes still doesn't make up for the tedium of constant travel.

Tim says the members of INXS go through periods of virtually ignoring the cities they pass through, and then periods when they make the effort to get out of the hotel and enjoy the sights.

'We used to travel in a bit of a bubble, that's true, but now we tend to think "fuck this, we're here, let's enjoy it". We do things together quite often, too, although if someone has their woman along with them, they'll go off and do things alone. Invariably I never have my wife

on the road. . .so I'll sometimes go and do things with the other chaps. We all love to shop for clothes, and I'll often try to look at a few antique shops as well.'

'One of the nicest things about touring for me is that it's not just the six of us in a room together', says Andrew. 'There are all these other people in the touring party that you can socialize with and on a long tour that can be a welcome relief. There are certainly days when we don't see each other or communicate in any way apart from the soundcheck and the gig.'

Perhaps the most difficult element of touring is fatigue. After months of constant performing and travelling, deprived of sleep and proper meals, tiredness can become a problem. As Garry Gary Beers puts it, 'you get to a point where you're conserving every ounce of energy just to play, sleep and eat.'

'We have very high expectations of ourselves', explains Jon. 'Particularly when a tour starts to drag on a bit we start to get very fatigued. . .and then we start to question whether we're maintaining our standards.'

'I really hate it when we all start to get exhausted', agrees Tim. 'We get very frustrated with ourselves because we feel as if we're not being entirely honest with the audience. I mean, you can only give so much. . .and then you feel as if you're just going through the motions a bit.

'We find as we get older that we're getting less and less interested in really long tours. We're going to try and keep tours shorter in future, because then you can still have fun.'

For Michael Hutchence, the years of touring with INXS have left one serious legacy – he has sustained considerable damage to his vocal chords. While most of this damage will eventually heal, it casts serious doubts on the likelihood of long-haul touring in the future.

When I had all the problems with my throat on the Australian tour I went to see a Sydney throat specialist who is one of the very best in the world', says Michael. 'He looked at my throat, and then he asked to see how much work I'd done over the past five years. So we pulled out a few bits of paper and showed him our touring itinerary since the mid-80s.

'He took one look at this and said I was incredibly lucky to have any voice left at all. He said what we'd done was ridiculous, and I think I agree with him.'

**Preparing for the Rock in Rio show, Brazil. Far left and top: Michael Hutchence and Andrew Farriss doing soundchecks. Above: Tim Farriss and Garry Gary Beers watching as it all starts to happen.**

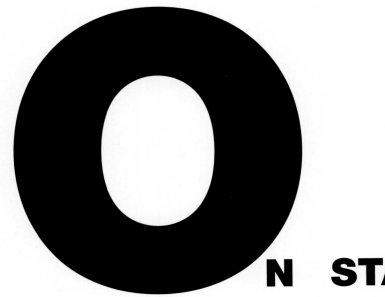

**O**N STAGE 'There was this theory going around for a while that the reason audiences keep getting bigger and bigger isn't because the band is better advertised or selling more records, but because it takes more and more people to contain you. So the performer gives out more and more and more...and the audience has to keep growing so they can catch it all. And of course as soon as you start to give out less...the audience will start to shrink.' (Michael Hutchence)▶

'We've had something like 2,500 rehearsals', says Kirk Pengilly, referring to the band's staggering record of live shows. 'After all those gigs, we'd like to think that we never put on a bad show these days. We've learnt how to pace ourselves and enjoy being there. Even if one of us isn't feeling that great I think we still do a pretty good show that the audience will enjoy.

'We're very conscious of the fact that with a band in our position every gig is important, every gig has to be professionally presented and as good as it can possibly be. Every one of us has their own needs, if you like – their own demands for time and space before a gig so that we'll all be in a position to meet that common goal. We've found that if we don't get that space then we may well blow the gig.'

The backstage scene before an INXS gig is about as far from old-style rock & roll excess as a band can possibly get. Along with vast road cases full of stage clothes and instruments, many members of the band travel with personal exercise equipment and weights to aid in the pre-show preparation.

'I treat gigs as being just like a very intense, demanding sport', says Garry Gary Beers. 'You get out there for two hours a night and work really hard. I promise you that I work up a bigger sweat on stage than I ever have playing squash or football. So we always have a masseur at hand and we have the exercise equipment backstage for loosening up, and what we seem to find is that everyone uses it for the first part of a tour, but as it drags on you slow down on that because you're basically trying to preserve your energy.

'You certainly don't find me partying before a show. I might have one or two drinks just to calm down a bit, but the thing about alcohol is if you drink too much you'll feel great for the first half hour, but then you start to feel terrible as it wears off, plus you start looking for a toilet. But honestly, performing live is a natural high. It

Left: Michael Hutchence before the show. Far left below: Tim Farriss joins the rhythm section at Melbourne Tennis Centre. Below: at Rock in Rio. Far left above: at Sydney Entertainment Centre after the show. Following pages: INXS in Europe with lighting effects by Roy Bennett.

gets the endorphins pumping and you don't need to suppress it with alcohol.'

'I'm not so big on the idea of the gig as sport', counters Michael Hutchence. 'Some people make such a fuss before a gig, like they're doing weights or pacing back and forth getting really worked up and going "woah! Yeah!". But I like trying to be really quiet before a gig. I like to feel the difference between being in a little room by myself and out in front of a huge crowd.'

On stage, the members of INXS try to have as much fun as possible. The hilarity often begins at the sound-check, with the band limbering up on off-the-wall cover versions.

'Yeah, we all love to jam on other people's songs during the soundchecks', confirms Garry. 'But for some reason we never seem to get around to putting them in the set – someone always goes cold on the idea. We actually do a great version of *It's Not Unusual* which we whipped up in Las Vegas. The very next night Tom Jones came to the show and we almost put it in the set – but Michael chickened out at the last minute.'

The band's live performances are clearly where singer

Michael Hutchence comes into his own. His ability to move large audiences and to provide a strong focal point on stage is extraordinary. Hutchence argues that he is no more important to the INXS live show than any other member, but he acknowledges that there is far more riding on his shoulders.

'I don't know that I have any more pressure than anyone else on stage', he says 'but the thing that can be a problem sometimes is that it's much more obvious if I'm having a bad night. One of the other guys can be feeling a bit ill and he can just stand there and play his instrument. Whereas I can't just do that. I've tried doing that a few times, saying to myself, "I'll just concentrate on the singing and I'll be fine", but that really isn't enough.

'I've set my own trap in a way. I might do a few really good shows early in the tour where something magic happens on stage, and then you're kind of bound to live up to that as often as you can.'

As Garry Gary Beers readily admits, playing live in INXS isn't all wine and roses. INXS may try to approach their shows with a sense of humour, but they also take their work very seriously indeed. After the shows, the band frequently engages in intense post-mortems.

'We had a rule, which lasted about one night, that we wouldn't discuss the show straight afterwards. It's hard straight after a gig, because your ears are still ringing and you're pumped up with adrenalin, so we can find ourselves standing around shouting at each other.

'Sometimes we get very critical about things because we're so passionate about what we do. It's something we've been doing together for half our lives, and although we're generally a pretty happy bunch there are times when things get pretty heated. But on the whole our discussions are very constructive. The idea is just to make the show as good as we possibly can.'

**Far left: Kirk Pengilly with his daughter April.**
**Left, above and below: Kirk switches roles and instruments easily.**
**Above: Garry Beers after the gig at Wembley Stadium.**

## The New Album

Almost as soon as the *X* tour was finished, the members of INXS began preparations for the recording of their eighth studio album. Andrew Farriss had already written a number of songs on the road – including *Shining Star*, which was added to the *Live Baby Live* album as a bonus track.. Back in Australia, the songwriting continued, with Andrew and Michael Hutchence sitting down to actively collaborate on songs for the first time in several years.

In November 1991 the band gathered in Sydney's Rhinocerous Studios to commence sessions for the new album. For the first time ever, INXS decided it was time to produce themselves, so with the help of Australian producer Mark Opitz (the man who had produced *Shabooh Shoobah* a decade before – and who had recorded and produced *Live Baby Live*) they commenced work in earnest. Almost as soon as the sessions began, it was apparent that the band's newfound sense of purpose and unity – so eloquently stated at Wembley Stadium – was translating into the studio.

'I think it's immediately obvious with this album that we've reached a whole new level,' says Kirk Pengilly. 'We're feeling very positive – and also very confident in our own abilities. This album hasn't been difficult at all – in fact we've had so many ideas it's just ridiculous. The motto for this album was "we'll try any idea" – and believe me, we have. I really think this album is going to shock a lot of people.'

The new album sees the band experimenting with a broad range of feels and approaches. From the sweeping power of songs like *Baby Don't Cry* and *Men and Women* (both recorded live-to-tape with the 65-piece Australian Concert Orchestra) to the confrontational attack of *Taste It,* this is an ambitious, wide-ranging album.

Michael Hutchence can only agree. 'It's been great to be in control of the album,' he says. 'We've always had a producer standing between us and the music, but with this one we've basically done whatever we wanted to do. We've got songs on this album that sound really weird and Indian – and we've got songs that sound really lush and European. We also have songs that are very intense and tough. It's a real mixture, but it works.'

The sessions for the new album were finalised in March 1992 and mixed by Bob Clearmountain in Los Angeles – and even while the last-minute touches were being added the good omens started to appear. First Garry Gary Beers and his wife Jodie gave birth to their first child – and then Jon Farriss capped off an exciting period of band harmony by getting married.

'These days we seem to progress even more from one album to the next,' observes Kirk. 'We realise that we're now in a position to try just about anything, to experiment with all sorts of things. We're not like a heavy metal band that can only do a small range of things – we feel as if we're working in a wide open space.

'So often the music industry wants to pigeon-hole music, and we've always confused people because we're not one simple thing. We're not easily tagged as a "rock band" or any other kind of band. There's really one word to describe us: INXS.'

# chronology

## 1977
Group formed as The Farriss Brothers in Sydney, Australia. Line-up is: Andrew Farriss, Jon Farriss, Tim Farriss, Michael Hutchence, Kirk Pengilly and Garry Gary Beers. Thirteen years later, personnel will be unchanged.

## 1978
Entire band moves from Sydney to Perth, a 3,279-kilometre journey across the Australian interior. The Farriss Brothers spend ten months writing, rehearsing and playing local hotels and mining towns.

## 1979
Returning to Sydney, group plays first inner city shows. Re-named INXS, they make live debut on September 1, at the Oceanview Hotel, Toukley.

## 1980
### MAY
First INXS single *Simple Simon We Are The Vegetables*, released in Australia by independent Deluxe Records. Also released in France.
### OCTOBER
Debut album, *INXS*, released in Australia, yields hit single, *Just Keep Walking*. Group tours East Coast extensively (Melbourne, Sydney, Brisbane), often playing seven nights a week..

## 1981
Cross-country touring of homeland begins in earnest. *Fear And Loathing Tour, The Campus Tour, Stay Young Tour, Tour With No Name* – some 300 shows altogether.
### MARCH
*The Loved One* single released in Australia, cover of Number 1 Australian hit by The Loved Ones, a top Melbourne band of the 60s (INXS will record song again in 1987 for *Kick* album).
### OCTOBER
Second album, *Underneath The Colours* released. Commercial and critical success, it reaches top 15 in Australian charts and includes the anthemic single, *Stay Young*.

## 1982
### JANUARY
INXS tours New Zealand for first time. Upon return to Australia, band records *The One Thing*, produced by Mark Opitz.
### APRIL
Andrew, Michael and Kirk embark on 'pilgrimage' to England and America.
### JUNE
Recording of third album begins, Mark Opitz producing.
### JULY
INXS signed to WEA Records for Australasia. *The One Thing* single released, goes to Top 15.
### OCTOBER
*Shabooh Shoobah* released in Australia, hits top five, becomes INXS third gold album down under. One critic comments,

'INXS have a definite style, an instantly recognizable sound that cannot be confused with any other band in the country.' Group performs nationwide on the 78-date *Una Brilliante Band De Musica Amenizara Espectaculo* tour.

## 1983
### JANUARY
INXS signed by Atlantic Records for North America.
### FEBRUARY
INXS makes North American debut with release of *The One Thing* single. Video enters high rotation on MTV; song hits US top 30.
*Shabooh Shoobah* released in US to wide acclaim.
*Rolling Stone* calls the album 'novel in approach and stirring in execution. . .amid the current plague of identical synth-pop records, *Shabooh Shoobah* is no ordinary song and dance.'
*Don't Change* is next radio/video favourite.
### MARCH
INXS begins marathon debut US tour.
### MAY
Band plays first New York City headlining show at The Ritz. Same month, appears at massive US Festival in California.
### AUGUST
Atlantic release *Dekadance*, mini-LP containing remixes of four songs from *Shabooh Shoobah*.
### SEPTEMBER
*Original Sin* recorded at New York's Power Station with Nile Rodgers producing, Daryl Hall and Dave Skinner on backing vocals.
Recording of fourth album begins at England's Manor Studios. Produced by Nick Launay, *The Swing* is completed in Australia in December.

## 1984
### JANUARY
*Original Sin* hits Number 1 in Australian charts. INXS plays sold-out tour of homeland.
### FEBRUARY
Band embarks on first full-fledged world tour. *The Swing* debuts at Number 1 in Australian charts.
### MAY
*The Swing* released in America. Debut London performance at The Astoria.
### JUNE
*Original Sin* goes to Number 1 in France.
### JULY
First albums, *INXS* and *Underneath The Colours*, released in US.
### SEPTEMBER
Three-month North American tour concludes with sold-out show at Hollywood Palladium.
INXS becomes first international group to play Guam.
### DECEMBER
*Original Sin* goes to Number 1 in Argentina.

## 1985
INXS performs for total of 50,000 people at three summer shows in Australia – including 20,000 at sold-out Adelaide

Football Park for Year of the Youth.

*The Swing* achieves double-platinum homeland sales, ranking as one of the five top-selling albums in Australian music history.

**MARCH**

INXS commences recording fifth album at Sydney's Rhinoceros studios with producer Chris Thomas.

**MAY**

Band wins unprecedented seven Countdown Awards (Australian equivalent of US Grammies).

**JULY**

INXS plays for Live Aid at Sydney's Entertainment Centre; performance is beamed around the world.

**AUGUST**

Work on new album, *Listen Like Thieves*, completed at Air Studios in London.

World Tour begins in Australia.

**OCTOBER**

*Listen Like Thieves* released. First US single, *This Time. Rolling Stone* enthuses, 'INXS rocks with passion and seals the deal with a backbeat that'll blackmail your feet.'

INXS tours South America.

**NOVEMBER**

Band returns briefly to Australia for Rockin' the Royals charity concert in the presence of Prince Charles and Princess Diana.

Headlining North American tour commences with string of sold-out shows along West Coast.

**DECEMBER**

Atlantic Video releases INXS long-term home video, *The Swing And Other Stories*.

INXS plays pair of SRO shows at New York's Beacon Theatre.

## 1986

**JANUARY**

*What You Need,* second single from *Listen Like Thieves,* released. INXS plays dates in New Zealand and Europe before returning to North America in early February.

**MARCH**

*Listen Like Thieves* certified RIAA gold in US and heads quickly towards platinum.

*What You Need* becomes band's first top ten single in America, continues on into top five. Band takes break to pursue individual projects: Michael Hutchence stars in film *Dogs In Space*, directed by Richard Lowenstein. Hutchence earns critical raves for movie debut, while soundtrack yields top ten solo hit, *Rooms For The Memory*. Andrew Farriss produces solo single for vocalist Jenny Morris (back-up singer on INXS tour) which hits Australian top ten and goes gold. Tim goes fishing.

In Australia, where *Thieves* goes triple platinum, INXS wins three more Countdown Awards.

**MAY**

INXS is back on the road for *If You Got It, Shake It* world tour.

**JUNE**

Band plays sold out show at London's Royal Albert Hall.

**JULY**

45-date North American tour begins: *Listen Like Thieves* yields new single *Kiss the Dirt (Falling Down The Mountain)*. INXS returns to Australia for triumphant *Si Lo Tienes Muevelo* tour. Jon

Farriss produces Richard Clapton, 'Godfather' of Australian rock & roll.

**OCTOBER**

Atlantic Video releases *What You Need* home video compilation.

## 1987

**JANUARY**

INXS headlines extraordinary *Australian Made* tour of homeland. With eight other Australian bands on bill, group plays for 200,000 fans across country; event preserved in film and book documentaries.

Recording of next album takes place at Rhinoceros in Sydney and Studio De La Grande Armée in Paris, with Chris Thomas again producing. Bob Clearmountain mixes at Air Studios in London.

**OCTOBER 16**

1987-88 *Calling All Nations* world tour commences in US.

**OCTOBER 19**

*Kick*, sixth INXS album, released. First North American leg runs through late November, followed by December tour of UK.

## 1988

**JANUARY**

*Kick* simultaneously certified RIAA gold and platinum. Album will pass quadruple-platinum mark in US sales. New album's first single, *Need You Tonight* becomes INXS first Number 1 US single. Spurred on by success of *Kick*, US catalogue sales soar: *The Swing* and *Shabooh Shoobah* certified RIAA gold; *Listen Like Thieves* certified RIAA platinum.

**MARCH**

US tour resumes. INXS plays three sold-out shows at Radio City Music Hall in New York City. Atlantic Video releases *Kick – The Video Flick* which will go platinum in US. Second single from *Kick*, *Devil Inside*, hits US top 5.

**MAY**

Third US leg of 1987-88 world tour begins. *New Sensation*, third *Kick* single, hits US top five.

**AUGUST**

Fourth US tour leg begins, included are trio of New York arena shows – Madison Square Garden, Meadowlands Arena, Nassau Coliseum.

*Kick* yields fourth single, *Never Tear Us Apart*.

**SEPTEMBER**

INXS sweeps MTV Video Music Awards. *Need You Tonight/ Mediate* clip wins in five categories: Best Video, Best Group Video, Best Editing, Breakthrough Video, Viewers' Choice.

US tour wraps up; INXS heads to Japan, then back to Australia for record-breaking homecoming tour.

## 1989

**JANUARY**

INXS earns first Grammy nomination for Best Rock Performance By A Group. Band also up for BP (UK) and Juno (Canada) awards.

After sixteen months on the road, INXS finally takes a break. During hiatus, individual projects include: Michael Hutchence records MAX Q album with Ollie Olsen. Acts in second feature film, playing poet Percy Synghe Shelley in Roger Corman's *Frankenstein Unbound*. Andrew Farriss produces Jenny Morris's second solo album, *Shiver*, which is certified Australian triple-platinum. Tim Farriss produces documentary on big game fishing, *Fish In Space*. Jon Farriss and Kirk Pengilly contribute to the music; Tim catches fish. Garry Gary Beers works with *Absent Friends*, co-producing album with band member Sean Kelly.

### NOVEMBER
INXS regroups to begin song rehearsals.

### DECEMBER
Band begins recording new album, with production once again by Chris Thomas (his third consecutive INXS project).

## 1990

### JANUARY
Following holiday break, INXS continues recording.

### MARCH
While group takes short hiatus from recording, Michael and Andrew write more songs. Jon does the same at home. Song rehearsals resume, followed by return to studio to complete recording of new album, later to be titled *X*.

### JUNE
Michael and Chris Thomas begin album mixing in London. Andrew plays live shows with Jenny Morris, including opening for Prince tour in France and Germany. Tim and Kirk produce Australian band *Crash Politics*.

### AUGUST
*Suicide Blonde*, first single from new album, released. Video is directed by Richard Lowenstein.

### SEPTEMBER 6
INXS live in Los Angeles on MTV Video Music Awards Show.

### SEPTEMBER 21
*X*, the seventh INXS album, released. Band prepares for 1990-91 world tour, set to commence in October.

### SEPTEMBER 24
*Suicide Blonde* reaches gold status in Australia.

### OCTOBER 1
INXS commences the *X* tour in the tropics of Northern Australia. Fans from all over Australia fly in to witness INXS first show in two years. *X* reaches platinum status in Australia upon first week of release.

### NOVEMBER 1
INXS commences European *X Factor* tour in Holland.

### NOVEMBER 28
INXS plays the first of four sell-out shows at London's Wembley Arena.

### DECEMBER 9
The trucks get stuck in blizzard conditions on their way to Glasgow SECC and for only the second time in the band's 10-year touring history, INXS is forced to cancel a show.

### DECEMBER 17
INXS completes the year by playing The Point Theatre, Dublin. This is the first of many shows to be recorded during the *X Factor* tour.

### DECEMBER 31
Westwood One run their INXS New Year's Eve special across North America.

## 1991

### JANUARY 12
INXS in Mexico play to 50,000 people, and 1,000 armed guards are brought in to contain the excited crowds. INXS is the first rock band to play in Mexico since The Doors nearly 20 years ago.

### JANUARY 19
INXS headlines Rock in Rio, Brazil to more than 100,000 people and then performs in Argentina.

### JANUARY 28
INXS performs the single *Disappear* on the American Music Awards.

### JANUARY 30
INXS performs on the Arsenio Hall Show.

### FEBRUARY 1
The American *X Factor* tour is launched in LA's famous Whiskey Au Go Go nightclub.

### FEBRUARY 9
INXS completes a week of television appearances by performing on *Saturday Night Live*.

### FEBRUARY 16
INXS plays to a sell-out crowd at Madison Square Gardens.

### FEBRUARY 22/23
INXS records their live performance at the Spectrum in Philadelphia for the *Live Baby Live* album.

### MARCH 11
Tickets go on sale for the Australian tour. A record-breaking 22,000 tickets are sold in 20 minutes in Sydney.

### MARCH 15/16
INXS record their two sell-out performances at Chicago's Rosemount for their live album.

### APRIL 4
*X* attains double platinum status in Australia.

### MAY 8
INXS completes the Australian tour ending at Sydney Entertainment Centre.

### MAY 9
Commenced research for mixing and co-producing *Live Baby Live* at Sydney's Rhinoceros Studios.

### JUNE 28
INXS returns to Europe and launches European tour at an unannounced Belgium club show.

### JUNE 29
INXS headlines Rock Am Ring Festival to 51,000 people in Cologne. This kicks off a series of festival shows throughout Europe including France, Holland and Switzerland.

### JULY 7
INXS plays their first ever show in the Eastern Bloc. The show takes place in Budapest, Hungary.

### JULY 13
INXS headlines *Summer XS* to a sell-out crowd of 72,000 people at Wembley Stadium. This is filmed by David Mallet (AC/DC, Madonna) for release on video to coincide with *Live Baby Live*.

### JULY 14
INXS records *Shining Star*, written by Andrew Farriss, in London.

### JULY 16
INXS finishes a 10-month world tour by playing a second night

at the Glasgow SECC, to make up for the show cancelled on December 9, 1990.

**AUGUST 16**
Completed mixing and co-producing with Mark Opitz *Live Baby Live* at Sydney's Rhinoceros Studios.

**OCTOBER 10/11**
Recorded video for *Shining Star* at Sydney's Phoenician Club.

Once again directed by David Mallet.

**OCTOBER 21**
*Shining Star*, the first single from *Live Baby Live* released.

**NOVEMBER 11**
*Live Baby Live* album and *Live Baby Live* video released.

# discography

## SINGLES

| | |
|---|---|
| Sep 1981 | Just Keep Walking/Scratch |
| Jun 1983 | Don't Change/You Never Used To Cry |
| Jun 1983 | Don't Change/You Never Used To Cry/Golden Playpen (12") |
| Sep 1983 | The One Thing/The Sax Thing |
| Sep 1983 | The One Thing/Black And White (12") |
| Sep 1983 | The One Thing/Black And White/Here It Comes II (12") |
| Feb 1984 | Original Sin/Jan's Song (live)/To Look At You (live) |
| Feb 1984 | Original Sin/Original Sin (extended version)/Jan's song (live)/To Look At You (live) (12") |
| May 1984 | I Send A Message/Mechanical |
| May 1984 | I Send A Message (long distance)/Mechanical/I Send A Message (localcall) (12") |
| Feb 1986 | This Time/Original Sin (long version) |
| Feb 1986 | This Time/Original Sin (long version)/Burn For You (extended version)/Dancing On The Jetty (doublepack single) |
| Feb 1986 | This Time/Original Sin/Burn For You/Dancing On The Jetty (12") |
| Apr 1986 | What You Need/Sweet As Sin |
| Apr 1986 | What You Need/Sweet As Sin/This Time/What You Need (live) I'm Over You |
| Apr 1986 | What You Need/Sweet As Sin/What You Need/The One Thing/Don't Change/Johnson's Aeroplane (2x12" doublepack) |
| Apr 1986 | What You Need (remix) Sweet As Sin/What You Need (live)/The One Thing (live) (12") |
| Jun 1986 | Listen Like Thieves/Begotten |
| Jun 1986 | Listen Like Thieves/Listen Like Thieves (instrumental)/Listen Like Thieves (live) Begotten (12") |
| Aug 1986 | Kiss The Dirt (Falling Down The Mountain)/Six Knots/The One Thing |
| Aug 1986 | Kiss The Dirt (Falling Down The Mountain)/Six Knots/The One Thing/Spy Of Love (12") |

| | |
|---|---|
| Aug 1986 | Kiss The Dirt (Falling Down The Mountain)/Six Knots/The One Thing/Original Sin/This Time (doublepack single) |
| Sep 1987 | Need You Tonight/I'm Coming (Home) |
| Sep 1987 | Need You Tonight/Mediate/I'm Coming (Home) (12") |
| Nov 1987 | New Sensation/Do What You Do |
| Nov 1987 | New Sensation/Do What You Do/Love Is (What I Say)/Same Direction (12") |
| Jan 1988 | New Sensation/Do What You Do (12" picture disc) |
| Jan 1988 | New Sensation/Do What You Do/Love Is (What I Say)/Same Direction (CD) |
| Feb 1988 | Devil Inside/On The Rocks |
| Feb 1988 | Devil Inside/On The Rocks/Devil Inside (7" version) (12") |
| Jun 1988 | Never Tear Us Apart (7") |
| Nov 1988 | Need You Tonight (7") |
| Apr 1989 | Mystify (7") |
| Aug 1990 | Suicide Blonde(7") |
| Nov 1990 | Disappear (7") |
| Mar 1991 | By My Side (7") |
| Jun 1991 | Bitter Tears (7") |
| Oct 1991 | Shining Star EP |

## ALBUMS

| | |
|---|---|
| Sep 1980 | Shabooh Shoobah |
| Mar 1982 | Underneath The Colours |
| July 1984 | The Swing |
| Feb 1986 | Listen Like Thieves |
| Nov 1987 | Kick |
| Sep 1990 | X |
| Nov 1991 | Live Baby Live |

# videography

**LONG-FORM VIDEOS**
INXS – The Swing & Other Stories
Living INXS
In Search Of Excellence
INXS – Kick Flick
INXS Greatest Video Hits
Live Baby Live

**PROMOTIONAL SINGLES VIDEOS**
Just Keep Walking
The Loved One
Stay Young
The One Thing
To Look At You
Spy Of Love
Don't Change
Original Sin
I Send A Message

Burn For You
Melting In The Sun
(Love Is) What I Say
Dancing On The Jetty
All The Voices
What You Need
This Time
Kiss The Dirt
Listen Like Thieves
Need You Tonight
Mediate

Devil Inside
New Sensation
Guns In The Sky
Never Tear Us Apart
Mystify
Suicide Blonde
Disappear
Bitter Tears
By My Side
Shining Star

# INXS X tour schedule 1990-1991

## October
Rehearsals – North Queensland
2 Mackay *Entertainment Centre*
3 Mackay *Entertainment Centre*
4 Mackay *Entertainment Centre*
5 Day off
6 Cairns *Kuranda Amp*
7 Cairns *Kuranda Amp*
8 Day off
9 Hervey Bay *Kondari Resort*
10 Hervey Bay *Kondari Resort*
11 Day off
12 Rockhampton *Music Bowl*
13 Townsville *Soundshell*

## November
Europe
1 Rotterdam *Ahoy*
2 Brussels *Forest National*
3 Day off
4 Day off
5 Zurich *Hallenstadion*
6 Frankfurt *Festhalle*
7 Day off
8 Copenhagen *Valby Hallen*
9 Stockholm *Globen*
10 Day off
11 Hamburg *Sporthalle*
12 Koln *Sporthalle*
13 Strasbourg *Hall Rhenus*
14 Day off
15 Montpellier *Zenith*
16 Bordeaux *Patinoire*
17 Toulouse *Palais Sports*
18 Day off
19 Madrid *Real Madrid Sports Hall*

20 Barcelona *Sports Palace*
21 Lyon *Palace Sports*
22 Milan *Palatrussardi*
23 Day off
24 Day off
25 London *Docklands Arena*
26 London *Docklands Arena*
27 Day off
28 London *Wembley Arena*
29 London *Wembley Arena*
30 London *Wembley Arena*

## December
1 London *Wembley Arena*
2 Day off
3 Birmingham *NEC*
4 Birmingham *NEC*
5 Birmingham *NEC*
6 Birmingham *NEC*
7 Day off
8 Day off
9 Glasgow *SECC (cancelled)*
10 Glasgow *SECC*
11 Manchester *GMEX*
12 Day off
13 Paris *Omnisport*
14 Brighton *The Brighton Centre*
15 Bournemouth *Bournemouth International Centre*
6 Day off
17 Dublin *The Point Theatre*
18 Dublin *The Point Theatre*

## January
The Americas
11 Arrive in Mexico City
12 Show Mexico *Palacio de los Deportes*

13  Show Mexico *Palacio de los Deportes*
14  Travel to Miami (holding options for Rio flight)
15  Day off
16  Day off
17  Rehearsal/Tech set up at hotel
18  Rio set up after 10pm for night focus
19  Rio show *Rock in Rio*
20  Travel to Buenos Aires
21  Set up Buenos Aires
22  Show Buenos Aires *The River Plate*
23  Travel to Uruguay midday: show cancelled
24  Travel to LA
25  Day off
26  Day off
27  Rehearse American Music Awards
28  American Music Awards Show Los Angeles *Universal Amphitheatre*
29  Day off
30  TV show *Arsenio Hall*
31  Band photo session (LA)

## February

1   Whiskey Au Go Go show (live radio)
2   Travel to Daytona, Florida
3   Daytona, Florida *Ocean Center*
4   Day off
5   Miami, Florida *Miami Arena*
6   Tampa, Florida *Sun Dome*
7   Rehearse *Saturday Night Live*
8   Atlanta, Georgia *Omni*
9   TV show *Saturday Night Live*
10  Day off
11  Day off
12  Dayton, Ohio *Hunter Center*
13  Pittsburgh, Pennsylvania *Civic Arena*
14  Buffalo, New York *Memorial Auditorium*
15  Day off
16  NYC, New York *Madison Square Garden*
17  Day off
18  Uniondale, New York *Nassau Coliseum*
19  Albany, New York *Knickerbocker Arena*
20  Day off
21  E. Rutherford, New Jersey *Meadowlands*
22  Philadelphia, Pennsylvania *Spectrum 1*
23  Philadelphia, Pennsylvania *Spectrum 2*
24  Day off
25  Worcester, Massachusetts *Centrum*
26  Hartford, Connecticut *Civic Center*
27  Syracuse, New York *War Memorial*
28  Day off

## March

1   Landover, Maryland *Capital Center*
2   Day off
3   Lexington, Kentucky *Rupp Arena*

4   Auburn Hills, Maine *Palace 1*
5   Auburn Hills, Maine *Palace 2*
6   Day off
7   Ottawa, Ontario *Civic Center*
8   Montreal, Quebec *Forum*
9   Toronto, Ontario *Maple Leaf Gardens*
10  Day off
11  Cleveland, Ohio *Richfield Coliseum*
12  Indianapolis, Indiana *Market Square Arena*
13  Day off
14  Milwaukee, Wisconsin *Bradley Center*
15  Chicago, Illinois *Rosemont Horizon 1*
16  Chicago, Illinois *Rosemont Horizon 2*
17  Champaign, Illinois *Assembley Hall*
18  Day off
19  Bloomington, Minnesota *Met Center*
20  Day off
21  Winnipeg, Manitoba *Convention Center*
22  Saskatoon, Saskatchewan *Saskatchewan Place*
23  Day off
24  Calgary, Alberta *Saddledome*
25  Edmonton, Alberta *Northlands Arena*
26  Day off
27  Vancouver, British Columbia *PNE Coliseum*
28  Seattle, Washington *Coliseum*
29  Portland, Oregon *Coliseum*
30  Day off
31  Salt Lake City, Utah *Salt Palace*

## April

1   Day off
2   Oakland, California *Arena*
3   Sacramento, California *Arco Arena*
4   Day off
5   Las Vegas, Nevada *Bally's*
6   Phoenix, Arizona *Desert Sky Pavilion*
7   Day off
8   San Diego California *Sports Arena*

Australia

9   Fly to Australia
10  In transit
11  Arrive Sydney
12  In Sydney
13  In Sydney
14  Travel to Perth
15  Perth *Entertainment Centre*
16  Perth *Entertainment Centre*
17  Day off
18  Day off
19  Adelaide *Memorial Drive*
20  Adelaide *Memorial Drive*
21  Adelaide *Rain Date*
22  Day off
23  Day off
24  Brisbane *Boondal Entertainment Centre*
25  Brisbane *Boondal Entertainment Centre*

26 Day off
27 Sydney *Entertainment Centre*
28 Sydney *Entertainment Centre*
29 Day off
30 Melbourne *Tennis Centre*

**May**

1 Melbourne *Tennis Centre*
2 Day off
3 Melbourne *Tennis Centre*
4 Melbourne *Tennis Centre*
5 Day off
6 Sydney *Entertainment Centre*
7 Sydney *Entertainment Centre*
8 Sydney *Entertainment Centre*

**June**

Europe
28 **Belgium – warm-up** *Vorhuit Club*

29 **Germany, Cologne** *Rock Am Ring Festival*
30 **France, Belfort** *Belfort Festival*

**July**

1 Day off
2 **Germany, Berlin** *Deutschlandhalle*
3 **Holland, The Hague** *Den Haag Statenhal*
4 **Holland, Maastricht** *MECC Maastricht*
5 Day off
6 **Austria, Vienna** *Casino Stadion*
7 **Hungary, Budapest** *Kis Stadion*
8 Day off
9 **Germany, Munich** *Olympiahalle*
10 **Switzerland, Lausanne** *Leysin Festival*
11 Day off
12 Day off
13 **UK, London** *Wembley Stadium*
14 Day off
15 **UK, Glasgow** *SECC*
16 **UK, Glasgow** *SECC*

# X tour set lists

### 1990 EUROPEAN TOUR
1. Suicide Blonde
2. Calling All Nations
3. Guns In The Sky
4. Hear That Sound
5. Wildlife
6. Bitter Tears
7. Need You Tonight/Mediate
8. Shine Like It Does
9. Faith
10. On My Way
11. Tiny Daggers
12. Know The Difference
13. Who Pays The Price
14. Listen Like Thieves/WAR
15. The Loved One
16. Lately
17. What You Need
18. New Sensation
19. Disappear
20. Kick
21. Devil Inside
Encore
22. The Stairs
23. Original Sin
24. Never Tear Us Apart
25. Don't Change

### 1990 US TOUR
1. Suicide Blonde
2. Calling All Nations
3. Guns In The Sky
4. Know The Difference
5. Hear That Sound
6. Wildlife
7. Bitter Tears
8. Need You Tonight/Mediate
9. Shine Like It Does
10. Faith
11. On My Way
12. Tiny Daggers
13. Who Pays The Price
14. Listen Like Thieves/WAR
15. The Loved One
16. Lately
17. What You Need
18. New Sensation
19. Disappear
20. Kick
21. Devil Inside
Encore
22. The Stairs
23. Original Sin
24. Never Tear Us Apart
25. Don't Change

### 1991 AUSTRALIAN TOUR
1. Suicide Blonde
2. Calling All Nations
3. Guns In The Sky
4. Hear That Sound
5. Wildlife
6. Need You Tonight
7. Mediate
8. By My Side
9. Mystify
10. Tiny Daggers
11. Know The Difference
12. Who Pays The Price
13. Disappear
14. Listen Like Thieves
15. The Loved One
16. Lately
17. What You Need
18. New Sensation
19. Kick
20. Devil Inside
21. The Stairs
22. Bitter Tears
Encore
23. Original Sin ( some shows)
24. Never Tear Us Apart
25. Don't Change

### 1991 EUROPEAN TOUR
1. Guns In The Sky
2. New Sensation
3. Send A Message
4. The Stairs
5. Know The Difference
6. Disappear
7. By My Side
8. Original Sin
9. Hear That Sound
10. Lately
11. The Loved One
12. One X One
13. Mystify
14. Bitter Tears
15. Suicide Blonde
16. What You Need
17. Kick
18. Need You Tonight/Mediate
Encore
19. Who Pays The Price
20. Devil Inside
21. Never Tear Us Apart